lucy

Jean Valentine

Quarternote Chapbook Series #8

Sarabande Books

LOUISVILLE, KENTUCKY

Managing Editor
Sarabande Books, Inc.
2234 Dundee Road, Suite 200
Louisville, KY 40205

Library of Congress Cataloging-in-Publication Data

Valentine, Jean.
  Lucy / by Jean Valentine. -- 1st ed.
    p. cm. -- (Quarternote chapbook series ; #8)
  ISBN 978-1-932511-68-0 (pbk. : acid-free paper)
  1. Lucy (Prehistoric hominid)--Poetry. I. Title.
  PS3572.A39L83 2009
  811'.54--dc22
                    2008032848

ISBN-13: 978-1-932511-68-0

Cover and text design by Kirkby Gann Tittle.

Manufactured in Canada.
This book is printed on acid-free paper.

Sarabande Books is a nonprofit literary organization.

 This project is supported in part by an award from the National Endowment for the Arts.

 The Kentucky Arts Council, the state arts agency, supports Sarabande Books with state tax dollars and federal funding from the National Endowment for the Arts, which believes that a great nation deserves great art.

Lucy, whose skeleton is approximately 3.2 million years old, whose genus and species are "*Australopithecus afarensis, or southern ape of Afar,* after the region of Ethiopia where the bones were found," was discovered in 1974, at Hadar in northern Ethiopia. "[...] Lucy remains the oldest and most complete adult human ancestor fully retrieved from African soil. . . . The Ethiopian people refer to her as *Dinkenesh,* an Amharic language term meaning *You are beautiful.*"

http://lucyexhibition.com

Lucy
your secret book
that you leaned over and wrote just in the dirt—
Not having to have an ending
Not having to last

. . . in thy book all my members
were written, which in continuance
were fashioned, when as yet there
was none of them.

Psalm 139:16

Two hands
were all you owned

for food
for love

Now you own none, Lucy
nor no words

only
breath marks

breath marks
only

nor no words
Or what *do* you do now Lucy

for love?
Your eye-holes.

Lucy
my saxifrage that splits the rocks
wildgood
mother
you fill my center-hole
with bliss
No one is so tender in her scream
Wants me so much
Not just, but brings me to be   Is
when I am close to death
and close to life

The spider
in her web three days
dead on the window Lucy

In the electricity of love, its lightning strike
or in its quiet hum in the thighs
like this little ice-box here
not knowing any better
or in the dumb hum of the heater going on
Little stirs in the room-tone
I rush outdoors into the air you are
Lucy
and you rush out to receive me
At last there you are
who I always *knew* was there
but almost died not
meeting
            when my scraped-out child died Lucy
you hold her, all the time.

Lucy
When the dark bodies
Dropped out of the towers

When Ruth died
And Grace
And Helen Ruth

And Iraq
And Iraq

And Nikolay

Lucy, when Jane in her last clothes
Goes across   with Chekhov
You are the ferryman, the monk
Ieronim
Who throws your weight on the rope.

I wash my plate and spoon
as carefully as a priest.
Did you have a cup, Lucy?
O God who transcends time,
Let Lucy have a cup.
You bodhisattva here-
with-us. You wanted to come back!
I'm afraid
and can't pay attention
to it   I'm
wild with heat and cold
and my head hurts:
The nine wild turkeys come up calmly to the porch
to see you, Lucy

My Work of Art
                    for Lucy

It's a piece of brown wrapping paper
taped to the wall   over the table
in this beautiful room with no pictures
First, written across the top:
"It was as if she was standing
across the road
waiting to see if anyone
wanted to get to know her."

Then taped under that:

Du der du weilst, und dessen weites Wissen

"You who know, and whose vast knowing
is born of poverty, abundance of poverty—

make it so the poor are no longer
despised and thrown away.

"Look at them standing about
    like wildflowers, which have nowhere else to grow."

Then a blue panther, a twenty-six cent stamp
from Florida, for postcards

Then a catalpa leaf curving
from its huge curving stem, the leaf

a little broken in its passing
from the West down to the East

and the note: I found this leaf
on my way to the Post Office.

Then Lucy you: hominid? sapiens?
sapere, to taste, be wise

Your skeleton
standing about, like a wildflower . . .

Lucy, what you want,
that I will do.
To hear you now.
Your poem. (But you need nothing.)

The deer and the wild turkeys
that draw close now to hear you.
My life is for.
In its language.
Your voice.

I can't tell cold from heat.
Anxiety
dust.
Death, no
not even dust.

Your Picture

Brown museum hair, brushed the way they brush it there,
brow lit from inside,
intelligent eyebrows,
a slightly wrinkly nose, a little flat—
brown woman, I want your nose, your
cheekbones of light—I was brown, I got white—
Your large and friendly mouth, half-open
in a half-smile,
like the Dalai Lama once, in a procession,
his smile "What am I doing here?"

But Lucy
your eyes.

So I gave all I had to the poor, standing about
like wildflowers.

Lucy,
the spider moved, last night,
and again, this morning . . .

I wonder Do you sleep and wake
where you are now? Do spiders
hibernate? Do they lay eggs
in webs on window-panes?

                    You must know
everything.

Enter the sweet Why
Don't entreat it
or question why
whistle why
whisper why
was sweetness done to you
done unto you
What I wanted most   the mother
has come to me
Will she stay in my ear? Lucy
Is it you?
Still all night long my
Lucy I entreat you
I will not let thee go except thou bless me.

Outsider Art

Martín Ramírez,
be with me!
"It looks just like a vagina,"
a bystander said. Yes
it is a vagina, with trains, and tunnels,
and like in the great cathedrals,
a clitoris, a starry one,
and a womb, jaunty Martín being born, Lucy
did you hear animal-woman
screams in the night?
Were you afraid?
Was it you last night
your scream over and over
as you give birth?

How did you pray, Lucy?
You *were* prayer.
Your hands and toes.
When writing came back to me
I prayed with lipstick
on the windshield
as I drove.
Newton made up with the world,
he had already turned himself
into gold, he was already there.

Skeleton Woman,
in   down
over   around

Blessing:
from the Old English *bletsian.*
Its root is the same as for blood.

My head is at your window, Lucy, at your glass,

But we offer nothing but money now,
we beam it to each other near and far,

But you are my skeleton mother,
I bring you
coffee in your cemetery bed.

This morning I miss most of all you, Martín,
and her who when you were born
looked and blessed your beauty.
Lucy, when you are with me
I feel the atoms
racing everywhere
in this old oak table,
in the eight-pointed double-star spider,
and in the starry rippling all around us.

Skeleton Woman, Guardian, Death Woman, Lucy,
Here, a picnic, corn bread, here, an orange
with Martín and me at the lip of the Earth Surface World.

NOTES

Page

4   The Holy Bible, King James Version

6   "my saxifrage that splits the rocks" from *A Sort of a Song* by
        William Carlos Williams: "Saxifrage is my flower that splits /
        the rocks." *The William Carlos Williams Reader,* New
        Directions, 1966.

8   Nikolay and Ieronim are in Chekhov's story *Easter Eve,* in *The
        Bishop and Other Stories,* translated by Constance Garnett, The
        Ecco Press, 1985.

10, 11 Rainer Maria Rilke, *The Book of Hours,* translated by Anita
        Barrows and Joanna Macy, Riverhead Trade, 2005.

16   Martín Ramírez was a Mexican immigrant painter who lived
        for more than thirty years in DeWitt State Hospital in
        California, until his death in 1963. His work was shown at The
        American Folk Art Museum in New York City in the spring of
        2007.

Heartfelt gratitude to Kaveh Bassiri, Kate and Max Greenstreet, Joan
Larkin, Jan Heller Levi, Jack Lynch, Anne Marie Macari, and Aaron
Smith; and to The MacDowell Colony, and to everyone at Sarabande
Books.

The Author

JEAN VALENTINE was born in Chicago, earned her B.A. from Radcliffe
College, and has lived most of her life in New York City. She won the
Yale Younger Poets Award for her first book, *Dream Barker,* in 1965.
Her collection *Door in the Mountain: New and Collected Poems
1965–2003,* was the winner of the 2004 National Book Award for
Poetry. Her work has also received a Guggenheim Fellowship and
awards from the NEA, The Bunting Institute, The Rockefeller
Foundation, The New York Council for the Arts, and The New York
Foundation for the Arts, as well as the Maurice English Prize, the
Teasdale Poetry Prize, The Poetry Society of America's Shelley
Memorial Prize, and the Morton Dauwen Zabel Award from the
American Academy of Arts and Letters.